NINJAGO™
Masters of Spinjitzu

NINJA HEROES

WRITTEN BY
BETH LANDIS HESTER

CONTENTS

INTRODUCTION

MEET AN UNBEATABLE TEAM OF NINJA.

The Ninja all have different personalities and they all bring their own strengths to the team. Friendship and teamwork are the greatest weapon the Ninja can wield against the forces of evil, and with their combined talents, they can take on any foe. The five noble Ninja also have many friends and allies who help them in their quest to protect Ninjago Island.

SENSEI WU

SENSEI WU IS dedicated to passing on his wisdom to a new generation. He believes that inner strength is as important as Spinjitzu skills, so training sessions always end with wise words for the Ninja and a cup of tea for him. Peaceful Wu uses his staff for just one cause: defending Ninjago.

THREE SUGARS, PLEASE!

Sensei Wu is always preparing a restorative cup of tea in his trademark blue teapot. He is rarely without a cup in hand as he watches over his pupils and instructs them in the ways of the Ninja.

> ## "THE BEST WAY TO DEFEAT YOUR ENEMY IS TO MAKE HIM YOUR FRIEND."
> ### SENSEI WU

Traditional conical hat shades eyes in heat of battle

DATA FILE

Known for:
Wisdom

Favorite weapon:
Staff of the Dragons

Likes:
Peace and quiet

Dislikes:
Cold tea

IS IT TEA TIME?

STYLISH SENSEI

Zane describes Wu's dark kimono as "most extraordinary," and he is right! Its golden symbols provide a powerful protection spell that once saved Wu from his evil brother, Garmadon. Wu still wears it today—being good never goes out of fashion.

DID YOU KNOW?

Sensei Wu is the son of the First Spinjitzu Master, the legendary hero who created Ninjago. Wu has vowed to uphold his father's legacy, and protect the land.

CALM TEACHER

Sensei Wu invites four young pupils to join his dojo in a remote monastery. He sees great potential in them, but knows they rely on him to provide structure, lessons, and a guiding hand if they are to unlock their true potential.

Shoulder armor provides much needed protection

WU THE WARRIOR

Peaceful, wise, old—these are all words that come to mind when the Ninja think of Sensei Wu. Don't underestimate this experienced fighter though; Wu's Spinjitzu moves are as sharp as ever!

Golden version of Wu's Nin-jo staff

Kai

BEFORE BECOMING THE Ninja of Fire, Kai used flames to forge weapons in his family's blacksmith shop. Now, Kai must learn to control his fiery temper and think before he leaps into action. Wu teaches him patience and red-hot Spinjitzu moves.

PROTECTIVE BROTHER

Kai's sister Nya is all the family Kai has got. Nya can stand up for herself, but Kai is determined to keep her safe. He even keeps a watchful eye on his friend Jay, who develops a crush on Nya.

I'M ON FIRE!

"THINK YOU CAN TAKE THE HEAT?"
KAI

Red face mask hides Kai's identity

DATA FILE

- ✹ **Known for:**
  Confidence, bravery
- ✗ **Favorite weapon:**
  Sword of Fire
- 👍 **Likes:**
  Action and excitement
- 👎 **Dislikes:**
  Losing at video games

OLD SCHOOL

High-tech gizmos and tricky computer code? No thanks! Kai's years in the blacksmith shop taught him to respect traditional weapons. He prefers blades and swords to buttons and switches any day (well, apart from video games).

MEETING WU

Kai meets Sensei Wu when the wise leader comes looking for a valuable map. It shows the hiding place of four powerful Golden Weapons that belonged to the First Spinjitzu Master. It has been hidden in Kai's blacksmith shop for many years.

Chart counts enemies defeated

Wide shields protect flanks

DID YOU KNOW?

Kai has a mysterious scar across one eye, from long before he became a Ninja. No one, not even his sister Nya, knows how he got it.

Golden blades fire forward

ROAD WARRIOR

Kai says he doesn't like technology, but when his elemental powers conjure this high-tech Blade Cycle, he can't wait to take it for a spin. With golden blades and scorching speed, this menacing machine has all the tools he needs to race after his enemies in a blaze of glory.

JAY

JAY IS FUN LOVING, fast-talking, and full of energy. He knows a witty one-liner is the perfect way to follow a Spinjitzu strike. That's not the only way Jay adds electricity: His lightning-fast reflexes and technical expertise are a serious asset to his team.

FAMILY RESEMBLANCE

Jay's parents, Ed and Edna Walker, turn other people's trash into cool inventions—including their customized clunker of a car, which they love taking out on adventures.

> "MIGHT AS WELL GO DOWN LAUGHING!"
>
> JAY

Yellow Techno Blade resembles a chainsaw

Robes have lightning strike decoration

DATA FILE

- ❋ **Known for:**
  Corny jokes
- ✕ **Favorite weapon:**
  Nunchucks of Lightning
- 👍 **Likes:**
  Hanging out with Nya
- 👎 **Dislikes:**
  Bad hair days

WHAT COULD GO WRONG?

AMAZING INVENTOR

Where others see sticks and paper, Jay sees a way to fly! Like his parents, handy Jay can turn odds and ends into amazing inventions. His creations have helped the Ninja out of countless scrapes, and a great imagination gives Jay the power to solve any problem.

STORM FIGHTER

In the cockpit of his super-fast plane, Ninja of Lightning Jay is a force of nature. The Storm Fighter has the power to attack as well as defenses to protect—if an enemy is on Jay's tail, he can streak away through the clouds like a lightning bolt!

Flight deck

DID YOU KNOW?
Jay was the first of the four Ninja to be found by Sensei Wu, and was the first to master Spinjitzu.

Slim fuselage for speed

SWEETHEARTS

On their first date, Jay tries to dazzle Nya with fancy clothes, a well-oiled hairdo, and partially true stories of his own incredible feats. But the pair really connect when Nya tells him the best true story of all: She likes him just the way he is!

LLOYD

LIKE HIS FATHER, Garmadon, Lloyd knows what it's like to be the bad guy. But when he begins to learn of his true potential, Lloyd discovers powers he never knew he had—including the power to choose his own amazing path and become a hero.

HOME SWEET HOME

The Ninja used Spinjitzu to stop Lloyd's evil plans, but his uncle, Sensei Wu, knows what Lloyd really needs to mend his ways: a kind welcome, a caring home, and a bedtime story or two.

> I'VE REALLY GOT MY HANDS FULL!

"NINJA NEVER QUIT."
LLOYD

Golden armor deflects enemy blows

Decorative Green Ninja insignia

DATA FILE

- **Known for:** Being the chosen Green Ninja
- **Favorite weapon:** Golden katanas
- **Likes:** Comic books
- **Dislikes:** Having to train all the time

DESTINY REVEALED

Few thought that a kid like Lloyd could become the powerful Green Ninja. But to everyone's surprise, he is revealed as the fabled hero when the Golden Weapons emit a green glow in his presence.

MY DAD COULD BEAT YOURS IN A FIGHT.

TROUBLED YOUTH

Lloyd once dreamed of an evil career just like his dad. After running away from the School for Bad Boys, he did his devious best to stir up trouble—teaming up with venomous snakes and trying to steal all the candy in Ninjago!

Green robes match the bike perfectly

COMPACT CYCLE

Lloyd's green cycle is small, but seriously speedy! The Green Ninja hops on and stands behind the steering controls to drive, but the bike's two wide tires provide plenty of balance to help keep him upright!

Sturdy suspension for a smooth ride

DID YOU KNOW?

Lloyd once used a magical elixir to defeat a monster, but it also changed him from a kid to a grownup.

NYA

SHE'S AN INVENTOR, navigator, and tech wiz—just not a Ninja. Sensei Wu did once ask Nya to join his dojo, but she is happy following her own path for now. She is still a key member of the team and often keeps the Ninja on track with her sensible advice.

DEFENDING HER TURF

Brave Nya never shies away from a challenge when her help is needed—like when she sails the Destiny Bounty through a terrifying storm! Nya's courage and skill prove she is every bit as tough as the boys

WATCH AND LEARN, BOYS!

"A GIRL'S GOT TO HAVE HER SECRETS!"
NYA

Handheld daggers can be thrown at enemies

Trousers under Nya's dress allow her to race into action

DATA FILE

- **Known for:** Amazing inventions
- **Favorite weapons:** Dagger and staff
- **Likes:** Cracking codes and solving mysteries
- **Dislikes:** Standing on the sidelines

SAMURAI BEATS NINJA EVERY TIME!

SECRET SAMURAI

While the Ninja are becoming famous in Ninjago, Nya trains in secret to become a powerful masked hero: Samurai X. Everyone is amazed at the power of the mysterious samurai, who can even outmaneuver the Ninja!

Mech even comes equipped with a cannon!

SAMURAI MECH

Her high-tech mech is just one of Nya's many cool inventions—but it sure is a showstopper! Towering over enemies, Nya can wield weapons, rescue allies, and even fly in this super-size armor.

DID YOU KNOW?

Although Nya appears to have inherited the same preference for red clothing as her brother Kai, her favorite color is blue... just like Jay's robes!

Phoenix symbol identifies the Samurai

COLE

THIS TOUGH GUY can lift heavy loads, throw massive objects, and lead his fellow Ninja through just about anything. But Cole, Ninja of Earth, is at his most powerful when he learns to mix his incredible strength with flexibility, an open mind, and some killer dance moves.

MUSCLE MAN

Some may like to lift weights, but with Cole's astonishing rock-hard muscles he can hoist a couple of friends—and their dinner—into the air! Cole is the strongest of the four Ninja, and can carry out amazing feats of strength.

> **"STAY STRONG. SHOW NO WEAKNESS."**
>
> COLE

Green Techno Blade is an unusual splash of color for Cole

Chain attached to blade's hilt can be used as a weapon

DATA FILE

- ✷ **Known for:**
  Strength and dependability
- ✗ **Favorite weapon:**
  Scythe of Quakes
- 👍 **Likes:**
  Mountain climbing
- 👎 **Dislikes:**
  Disloyalty and snakes

ROCKY AND COLE

Cole can't stand dragons—or at least that's what he thought until he had one of his own. With Earth Dragon Rocky, Cole is like a doting dad: showering his beloved dragon with affection and snacks, and even ordering him special treats in the mail.

Drill is powered by a powerful motor

EARTH DRILLER

Sensible Cole is always down-to-earth, but in his Earth Driller he even powers through it! The giant drill on the front of his vehicle can tunnel through immense obstacles. Despite its size, the speedy Driller can still leave enemies spluttering in its dusty tracks.

DID YOU KNOW?
Cole is a dance champ! His signature move is the Triple Tiger Sashay—a tricky aerial feat that amazes dance fans (including Cole's dad).

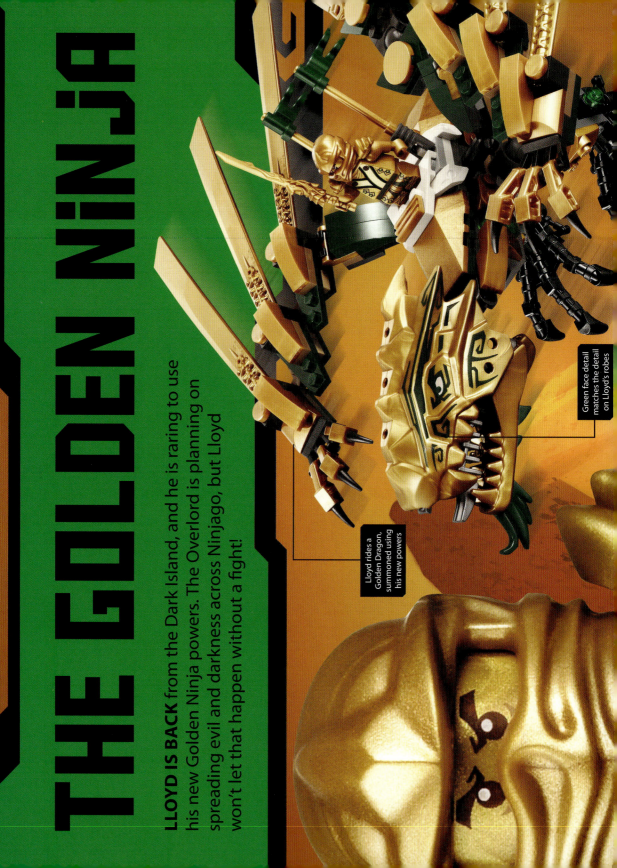

THE GOLDEN NINJA

LLOYD IS BACK from the Dark Island, and he is raring to use his new Golden Ninja powers. The Overlord is planning on spreading evil and darkness across Ninjago, but Lloyd won't let that happen without a fight!

Lloyd rides a Golden Dragon, summoned using his new powers

Green face detail matches the detail on Lloyd's robes

GOLDEN BOY

No ordinary weapon can defeat the Overlord. Lloyd uses his new powers to conjure a spinning ball of light and summon a magical Golden Dragon to help destroy the villain.

ENDLESS ARMY

The Ninja are hopelessly outnumbered as the vast Stone Army closes in on them. They are relying on Lloyd's new powers to save Ninjago... but will he be strong enough?

LIGHT RETURNS

Lloyd is victorious! Defeating the Overlord causes the evil that had infected Ninjago to disperse. The dark shadows lift and all is well again.

GOOD GARMADON

As light returns to Ninjago, those corrupted by evil are cured. Lloyd gets a reward more valuable than gold—the return of his father. Without evil, Garmadon is once again simply Lloyd's dad. He is unrecognizable!

Pure gold shoulder armor

Even Lloyd's hands are awash with golden energy

ZANE

WITH A MYSTERIOUS past and some odd ways, Zane has always been a little different. But there is more to this Ninja than even his closest friends suspect. Inside, he is a robot! His fellow Ninja still consider Zane a true brother, despite his high-tech circuitry.

SNACK TIME

When raiding the fridge for a midnight snack, only Zane climbs right in to eat his sandwich on the top shelf! The cold isn't a problem for the Ninja of Ice. But for his fellow Ninja, it can be a shock to find their friend sitting next to the cheese.

> ## "IT'S iCE TO SEE YOU."
> ### ZANE

Zane's Techno Blade glows icy blue when powered up

DID YOU KNOW?
Nindroid Zane can record sound, figure out the odds of victory, and stay underwater for more than ten minutes.

DATA FILE

❄ **Known for:**
Oddball ways

⚔ **Favorite weapon:**
Shurikens of Ice

👍 **Likes:**
Cold hard facts

👎 **Dislikes:**
Rusty joints

Snowy white robes never get dirty

FUNNY MAN?

When ultra-serious Zane discovered the switch that reactivated his memory, he also found a way to switch on his sense of humor—and launched into a hilarious song-and-dance routine!

> LOGICALLY, I AM THE COOLEST OF THE NINJA.

FALCON FRIEND

Master inventor Dr. Julien built Zane and his trusty mechanical falcon. This robotic bird becomes a trusted friend and guide. Zane can even tap into the falcon's vision to see distant enemies.

SPEEDING SNOWMOBILE

When he learns to focus his elemental power, Zane can create this machine out of thin air. With the Ninja of Ice on its back, the powerful snowmobile speeds across the snow, shooting enemies with devastating blasts of ice.

Icicle decorations match Zane's frosty powers

BUILDING ZANE

AN ADVANCED MACHINE like Zane takes plenty of planning, a good dose of tinkering, and a brilliant mind like Dr. Julien's to bring it all to life.

NINJA MASK

Dr. Julien could have included a built-in mask—but this removable design lets Zane keep a more human appearance.

OCULAR PROCESSOR

Regular people would call this an eye—but the instrument Zane uses to see can also record, scan, and analyze just like a computer.

CIRCUITS AND SWITCHES

A hinged door in Zane's chest makes it easy to access his inner workings. Inside are a number of switches that control Zane's programming.

CONTROL PANEL

All Zane needs to do to quickly access his settings is flip open his sleeve and—tada!—a switchboard. Perfect for a mid-battle upgrade!

HEAD TO TOE

Zane is unusual in many ways but with his standard head-to-toe measurement, he is exactly the same height as the other Ninja.

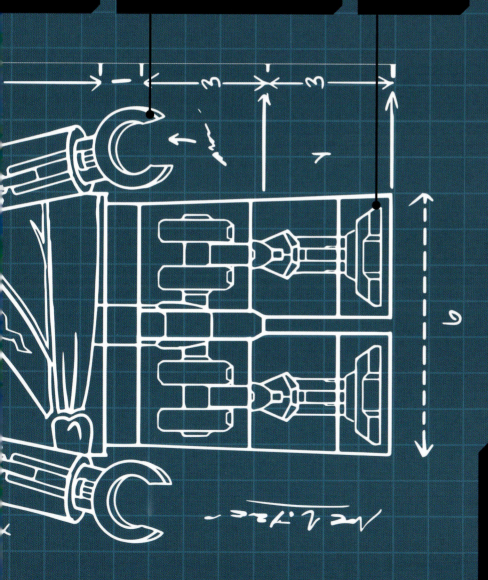

DEFAULT SETTINGS

		ON	OFF			ON	OFF		
POWER SOURCE:	EXTENSION CORD	☒		SENSE OF HUMOR:		☒	☑	OPTIONAL ABILITIES:	BREATHING UNDERWATER ☑
	BATTERY	☒							FLIGHT ☒
	ENHANCED CORE	☑		SINGING ABILITY:		☒	☑		DANCE SKILLS ☑
MEMORY:	ON	☒							GENEROSITY ☑
	OFF	☑		FRIENDSHIP FUNCTION:		☑	☒		FIGHTING SKILL ☑
									FASHION SENSE ☒

P.I.X.A.L.

WHAT DOES GENIUS Ninjago inventor, Cyrus Borg, do when he needs the perfect assistant? He builds one, of course! The result: a completely personalized Nindroid named Primary Interactive X-ternal Assistant Life-form—or P.I.X.A.L. for short.

SWEET 16
The P.I.X.A.L. we know wasn't the first: It took 16 tries for Cyrus to work out some of her design kinks, including an emotion suppressor that's still not quite perfect.

> HOW CAN I BE OF ASSISTANCE?

"I AM NOT BUILT FOR STEALTH."
P.I.X.A.L.

DATA FILE

- ❄ **Known for:** Analytical abilities
- ✕ **Favorite weapon:** Technical know-how
- 🖐 **Likes:** Being helpful— especially to Zane!
- 👎 **Dislikes:** Computer malfunctions

Exposed circuitry is visible under purple robes

COMPUTER GIRL

P.I.X.A.L. has amazing computing abilities—she can calculate huge sums, access endless facts, and make logical, data-based choices. P.I.X.A.L.'s programming also determines whether she is good or bad. She has cheerful green eyes when she is good, but watch out when they switch to red!

NINJA ALLY

P.I.X.A.L. is built to be helpful—and when her friends the Ninja are under attack, she does what she can to help. She knows she is not built for battle, but she has a few moves!

DID YOU KNOW?

P.I.X.A.L.'s programming means that computer viruses and power outages can cause her to glitch or shut down completely.

Central spinning rotor provides lift

P.I.X.A.L. sits in the front seat

PERFECT CO-PILOT

P.I.X.A.L. puts her amazing skills to good use when helping pilot Zane's Ninjacopter. With Zane at the controls, P.I.X.A.L. keeps careful watch over the flashing control panel.

HERO'S HONOR

The Ninja last saw Zane in battle, when his brave actions overpowered the Overlord—but also overloaded his own circuits. This statue of Zane was built in Ninjago, in his memory.

DID YOU KNOW?

Zane was captured by Master Chen while trying to find his fellow Ninja. After his own capture, Cole is the first Ninja to discover Zane 2.0.

NINJA

ZANE SACRIFICED HIMSELF during the battle against the Overlord. His Ninja friends never gave up hope they would see him again... but they never expected this rebooted new version!

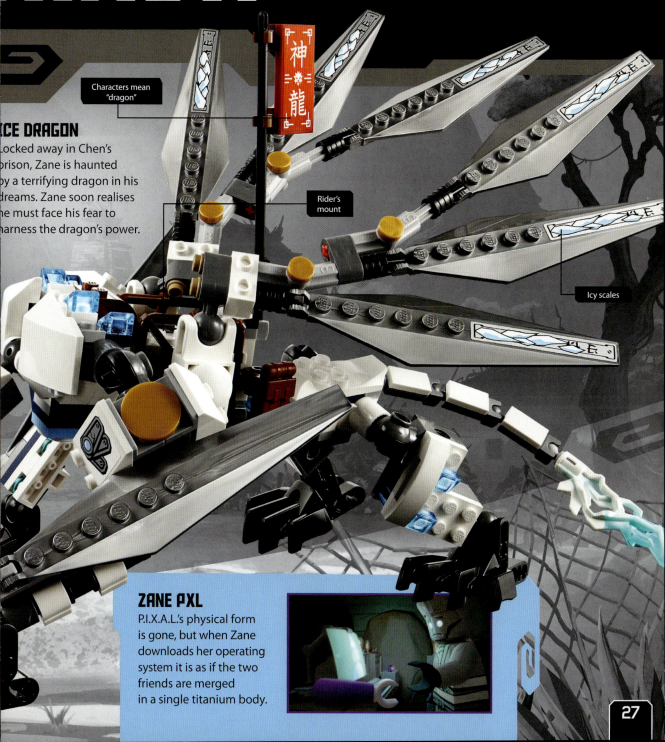

Characters mean "dragon"

ICE DRAGON

Locked away in Chen's prison, Zane is haunted by a terrifying dragon in his dreams. Zane soon realises he must face his fear to harness the dragon's power.

Rider's mount

Icy scales

ZANE PXL

P.I.X.A.L.'s physical form is gone, but when Zane downloads her operating system it is as if the two friends are merged in a single titanium body.

DK | Penguin Random House

EDITORS Pamela Afram, Matt Jones,
Clare Millar, Rosie Peet
SENIOR DESIGNERS Jo Connor, David McDonald
SENIOR SLIPCASE DESIGNER Mark Penfound
EDITORIAL ASSISTANT Beth Davies
DESIGNED BY Dynamo
COVER DESIGNER Stefan Georgiou
PRE-PRODUCTION PRODUCER Kavita Varma
SENIOR PRODUCER Lloyd Robertson
MANAGING EDITOR Paula Regan
DESIGN MANAGER Guy Harvey
CREATIVE MANAGER Sarah Harland
ART DIRECTOR Lisa Lanzarini
PUBLISHER Julie Ferris
PUBLISHING DIRECTOR Simon Beecroft

Additional photography by Gary Ombler

Dorling Kindersley would like to thank:
Heike Bornhausen, Randi Sørensen,
Martin Leighton and Paul Hansford
at the LEGO Group; Radhika Banerjee, Jon Hall,
and Pamela Shiels at DK for design assistance.

First American Edition, 2016
Published in the United States by DK Publishing
345 Hudson Street, New York, New York 10014
DK, a Division of Penguin Random House LLC

www.LEGO.com/ninjago
www.dk.com

A WORLD OF IDEAS:
SEE ALL THERE IS TO KNOW

Contains content previously published in LEGO®
NINJAGO™ Secret World of the Ninja (2015)

001-298874-Jul/2016

Page design copyright © 2016 Dorling Kindersley Limited

A catalog record for this book is available from
the Library of Congress.

ISBN: 978-5-0010-1403-4

Printed in China